IMAGES OF THE PAST

BRITISH SEASIDE

IMAGES OF THE PAST

BRITISH SEASIDE

LUCINDA GOSLING

First published in Great Britain in 2017 by
PEN & SWORD HISTORY
an imprint of
Pen & Sword Books Ltd,
47 Church Street,
Barnsley,
South Yorkshire,
S70 2AS

A CIP record for this book is available from the British Library.

ISBN 978 1 47386 215 9

Printed and bound in India by Replika Press Pvt. Ltd.

Pen & Sword Books Ltd incorporates the Imprints of Pen & Sword Aviation, Pen & Sword Maritime, Pen & Sword Military, Wharncliffe Local History, Pen & Sword Select, Pen & Sword Military Classics and Leo Cooper.

For a complete list of Pen & Sword titles please contact
Pen & Sword Books Limited
47 Church Street, Barnsley, South Yorkshire, S70 2AS, England

E-mail: enquiries@pen-and-sword.co.uk
Website: www.pen-and-sword.co.uk

Contents

Photographic film wallet advertising Kodak Film, with a seaside-themed cover illustration on the packaging.

Introduction

My Dear May

I hope you are quite well. I was paddling today and wish you were here and Mother brought me a spade and bucket.

With best love and kisses, Rosie

(Inscription on a postcard sent to Hendon from Hastings, 1906)

In a corner of the archive at Mary Evans Picture Library, housed on shelves extending high beyond reach, sit the library's collection of postcards. Neatly ordered alphabetically in landscape format files, they cover myriad subjects but, perhaps unsurprisingly, a substantial number contain seaside picture postcards, hundreds of them in fact. Roughly spanning the early 1900s to the mid-20th century, they were originally acquired for their pictorial content – beach scenes, ornate pier architecture, manicured gardens, lidos, funfairs, elegant seafronts, funicular railways or helter-skelters. But turn many of them over, and the original messages bring colour and life to the black and white photographs on the other side.

On a postcard sent to Deganwy in North Wales, dated 1921: *I am writing this card on the front at Torquay. It is a lovely spot. We have spent the afternoon here. I hope you are having the same kind of weather as we are. All that we could desire, love from Elsie.*

Another sent to Mrs Anderton of Sheffield from Ethel who was staying in Morecambe in 1910: *Oh! It is lovely here – wish I could stay a month. Am just off on the prom again. Hope you like this pc.*

Pip, staying in Selsey-on-Sea in West Sussex in 1936 seemed very happy with the sleepy town: *Dear Wen and Frank, We are spending a very nice holiday here. We have a nice, little bungalow and we are having a real lazy time. Plenty of bathing. It is very quiet here + nothing to do but it is just what we like. A nice free + easy time + just please ourselves. Haven't the dog with us. Hope you are both well.*

A postcard from Southsea sent to a Miss E. M. Petrie in Newcastle pulls hard at the heartstrings, written as it was by a father far from home in October 1917 during the Great War: *I was at Southsea last night but there were no little boys and girls on the beach. It is far too cold to wade or sit on the gravel at this time of year. This photograph must have been taken in the summer when the sun was shining. I have looked all over this picture but can neither find Mammy nor you. Can you find me? Eight kisses from Daddy*

Just a handful of missives from past, but they speak volumes of how the British seaside holiday had become imbedded in the national routine. The seaside might have been visited just once or twice a year by most of the early 20th century population, but it was something both familiar and special, from the unique parlance and activities such as 'going on the prom' to the varied ingredients that gave each resort its character. Before the advent of cheap air travel and the lure of Mediterranean sunshine in the 1960s, the British seaside was the very definition of a holiday for the vast majority.

Until the 18th century, Britain's coast was associated with fishing industries or ports, but the belief of doctors that sea-bathing was efficacious to the health began to see certain towns grow a modest tourist industry as spa town habitués gradually migrated to places such as Brighton, Weymouth and Sidmouth on the south coast. The sea may have been the main draw but soon genteel amusements – assembly rooms, landscaped parks and gardens and theatres – opened nearby to offer visitors a more rounded variety of entertainment while there. The arrival of the railways in the 1840s made the scenic towns around the coast far more accessible, but it was not until the Bank Holiday Act of 1871, when workers enjoyed a day of freedom on the first Monday in August, that the seaside was opened up to a wider demographic. Rapid growth in the late 19th century saw hotels and guest houses built, pleasure piers rise from the water, amusement parks, gardens, eateries, theatres, boating lakes and wide esplanades created specifically to cater to the tastes of the crowds who had begun to flock there, as well as retain their loyalty with each resort rivalling the other to offer the most tempting range of attractions. They were all components which, by the turn of the twentieth century, had lent these places the characteristic appearance and atmosphere of the seaside.

It is notable that the seaside, which grew and flourished from the late 19th century into 1960s, coincided with the development and adoption of photography. High days and holidays require documentation after all; proof of having been there, lasting memories to share with others. The images within this book are taken from the archives of Mary Evans Picture Library, with picture postcards, informal snaps and ephemera pulled together to tell the story of the seaside. With a strength in social history, the library's collection on the subject ranges from Blackpool Tower ballroom programmes and saucy seaside postcards, to scenic views and family photographs. It is the latter that are perhaps the most engaging. While some seaside resorts may have changed beyond recognition and others have fallen into decline, for anyone who enjoys a day at the seaside, many of the activities captured for posterity connect us with previous generations. The simple pleasures of sitting on the beach, gathering shells, digging or building sandcastles, turning up a trouser leg and going for a paddle – all of these have been the delight of daytrippers and holidaymakers through the years, each footprint in the sand washed away by the incoming tide. The pictures in this book remind us not only of how much has changed, but how much has also remained the same.

The Beach

'Sand in the sandwiches, wasps in the tea,

Sun on our bathing dresses heavy with the wet'

When John Betjeman wrote these two lines in his poem, 'Trebetherick', he conjured up the typical childhood experience of the British seaside. The beach, after all, IS the seaside and it is where holidaymakers and day trippers all eventually gravitate, staking out their place on sand or pebbles with picnic rugs, striped wind breakers, buckets, spades, towels and thermos flasks, settling down to enjoy the novelty of sand, sea and, occasionally, sun.

Charles Dickens, writing in 1851, understood well how the sandy, crescent-shaped beach of his native Broadstairs provided infinite amusement for children. 'The sands are the children's greatest resorts. They cluster there, like ants; burying their particular friends, and making castles with infinite labour which the next tide overthrows…' Jane Austen, on visiting the coast for the first time , stood on the beach and wept, overawed by the sheer novelty of seeing the swell of the sea.

Since that time, generations of children have enjoyed the same pleasures – sandcastle building, paddling, poking around in rock pools, hunting for shells or riding docile donkeys – giving the beach of the British seaside a wholesome and hallowed status compared to the tawdry amusement arcades and showy piers nearby. A day on the beach is a day of fresh air and exercise, of curiosity and discovery; a place where the days are long and routine is forgotten.

And while children play, parents relax in deckchairs in between bursts of activity - distributing (sandy) sandwiches, towelling down wet and shivering children or handing out pennies for ice creams. There may be many parallels between today's seaside visitors and those of the previous century, but sartorial choices were acutely different. On a sunny day in the 1920s, children in knitted, saggy swimsuits sit alongside grandfathers looking perfectly at ease in a three piece wool suit, tie and flat cap, while despite the advent of sunbathing and modern swimwear in the 1930s, members of the older generation sit in sweltering sunshine with newspapers or handkerchiefs as makeshift sun protection.

The beach may provide natural amusements, but that did not deter others from providing more. The images in this chapter depict pianists and Punch and Judy shows, ice cream sellers, beach cars, rides on docile donkeys and even a church service for children. With such an array of services on offer, it is no surprise that many visitors to the beach settled down for the day and only began to disperse with the incoming tide or setting sun.

Three ice cream fans on an unidentified beach, c.1930. Note the men in the background dressed in full suits. For working class day-trippers, their best suit would be their outfit of choice. Shorts and leisure wear were still the preserve of the well-off.

Ice cream cart on Blackpool beach, c.1950.

Lady posing for photograph on Brighton beach riding a 'prop' motorcycle c.1925. Just behind her, a wooden ice cream and drinks hut.

A family setting up a comfortable picnic area with the help of their removable car seats on Hayling Island in 1936. More remote coastal locations necessitated the use of a car and were more likely to be visited by middle class families seeking solitude away from the seething masses at popular resorts such as Blackpool, Southend and Margate.

Sitting out on a beach when the weather is less than clement seems a peculiar pastime but one practised with some frequency by the British over the years. Here, a couple enjoy a picnic on a pebble beach, using a fishing boat as a shelter from the stiff breeze.

Children fish for shrimps in the rock pools on Hunstanton beach in Norfolk in 1905.

Two ladies of a certain age bask in the sunshine in deckchairs on the beach in Blackpool, Lancashire, protecting their heads from the sun's rays with some fetching string vests. 1970.

The humble handkerchief as a sun hat in Blackpool, c.1950

Sunbathers on the beach at Shanklin, Isle of Wight in 1936. The increasing popularity of tanning during the 1930s led to backless swimsuit designs and the introduction of a number of tanning oils and creams to expedite the browning process.

A children's church service on the sands at the seaside – possibly at Llandudno, North Wales, 1902.

Ball games on the beach, 1920s. A family pose for a photograph on the beach at Weston-super-Mare in front of the Grand Pier accompanied by a variety of beach toys: cricket bat and stumps, a racquet and ball, bucket and spades. Father smokes a pipe.

On the beach at Margate: three ladies sit in deckchairs, while two boys in bathing costumes are relegated to the sand, though one sits astride a toy bulldog. 1920s.

Three 'thoroughly modern' girls in their swimming costumes, taking a ride on 'Wilfred' and 'Squeak', two donkeys, on the beach at Ramsgate, Kent. 1920s.

'Tent-land' — dotted with jolly striped tents to provide shelter and changing facilities, on the beach at Hornsea, Humberside, c.1910.

Ice cream on the beach, c.1930s

Prams on Brighton's pebble beach in the early 1960s.

Sandcastle construction under the pier at Ryde, Isle of Wight, 1930s.

Riding on the donkeys at Llandudno beach, Wales, early 1960s.

Impressive sandy fortifications at Weymouth, Dorset in a photograph by Roger Mayne from 1958.
The wide golden sands and shallow waters of Weymouth have made it popular since the
eighteenth century with sea bathers. Its popularity was kindled by King George III, who frequently
visited when seeking 'the cure' declaring it his 'first resort'.

Sunbather in Blackpool, 1970, clearly preparing for a big night out with her hair rollers in place!

A horse-drawn cart ride along the beach at Skegness, flanked by a number of paddlers, is one of the beach amusements on offer to visitors in 1910.

An overly faithful yellow Labrador sits on top of a sunbather at Abersoch, North Wales in 1968. Note the dapper chap in a suit sucking on his pipe and reading the papers nearby.

Playing with toy boats in a pool of seawater in Padstow Harbour at low tide. Padstow has been a thriving fishing harbour since the sixteenth century and enjoyed a modest influx of tourism from 1899 when the 'Atlantic Express' railway linked it to London. In recent years, the various restaurants opened by celebrity chef Rick Stein have put Padstow on the culinary map, attracting foodies from around the country.

SUMMER HOLIDAYS
in the British Isles

NEW SERIES, No. 1   1955

COOKS WORLD TRAVEL SERVICE

Sand, water, bucket and spade. A 1955 Thomas Cook brochure for holidays around the British Isles extolls the simple pleasures of the beach with their front cover photograph.

Donkey rides on Barry Island, South Wales in 1910. Barry Island, on the Bristol Channel, was connected with the mainland in 1896 via a 250m long pier. By the 1930s, its fairground was attracting over 400,000 visitors over a bank holiday weekend.

A family of five on holiday in the 1920s. Mother and father sit on deckchairs in their Sunday best.

Holidaymakers admiring a fantastic sandcastle made by the family seated within its walls, c.1919.

Small girl in a knitted swimsuit. Until the introduction of more modern, manmade textiles, swimwear and sunsuits were often knitted from wool and were prone to sag and itch when wet.

Relaxing in the sun on the beach at Hastings in June 1927. Like so many of the men in these photographs, this chap is wearing a full suit. The girl in the middle, however, is dressed in a summery ensemble with fashionable bandeau headband.

A large family group on an outing to Bexhill-on-Sea, East Sussex, 1932. Again, the men are in suits while the children are in summer dresses and shorts. The gentleman at the front however has taken off his socks and shoes – his one concession to the warm weather.

Beach tents provided shelter as well as somewhere to store belongings and change into swimwear. Unidentified British resort, 1920s.

Three women, dressed in hiking outfits, enjoy a beach picnic on Brean Sands near Weston-Super-Mare, Somerset in the 1930s. The ubiquitous cup of tea takes centre stage.

Beach pyjamas – wide legged palazzo pants worn with a short waistcoat or bolero, became popular during the late 1920s and early 1930s. Originally adopted by the society fashionistas of the French Riviera and Venetian Lido, this lady on an unidentified British beach looks as if her outfit – complete with matching accessories – might be homemade.

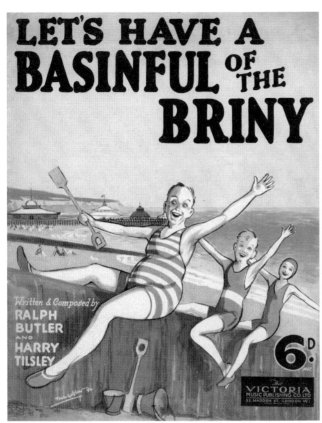

Beach-themed music cover from 1934 published by the Victoria Music Publishing Company.

An alternative to a castle for this group of children, who set sail in a sand boat. Unidentified location, 1920s.

Sandcastle-building competition 1913, organised by *Answers* Magazine at Brighton.

The artist Helen Allingham (1848-1926) pictured idyllic visions of rapidly disappearing villages, thatched cottages and country gardens around Victorian Britain. This painting, taken from her 1903 book, *Happy England*, depicted her own children riding in a goat cart on Broadstairs beach in East Kent.

Ambitious sandcastle building on Cooden Sands, near Bexhill, Sussex, c.1930.

A postcard from Milford-on-Sea, near Lymington, Hampshire, England, 1934.

The two most important accessories of any beach trip – a bucket and a spade. In this case, a lovely example of a decorated tin bucket. 1920s.

Dressed up for a day at the beach in the 1930s, but allowing feet and ankles some exposure to the fresh air.

Messing about in boats, 1950s.

Family on holiday at Lytham St Annes, Lancashire, 1915; the adults sitting in substantial-looking wickerwork beach chairs.

Boys wearing oilcloth overalls, perfect for dirty work. 1920s.

CHAPTER TWO

Entertainment

It may have been the sea, sand and fresh air that first lured visitors to the coast, but seaside towns soon sought to capitalise on the influx of leisure-seeking crowds, enticing them to linger longer, spend more and return again and again. Competition was rife between resorts to provide the most tempting range of amusements and entertainment. No commercial stone was left unturned. While vendors of sweets, lemonade, ice cream, seafood and fruit patrolled the beach hawking their wares and Punch and Judy stands could set up wherever there was an audience, more ambitious entrepreneurs built enormous complexes designed to ensure holidaymakers would never be bored. The late Victorian and Edwardian eras were a time of particularly rapid expansion with more and more buildings dedicated to pleasure. The Tower Ballroom in Blackpool, Southend's Kursaal, Whitley Bay's Spanish City and Margate's Dreamland were just a few of the iconic entertainment venues built to meet the demands and secure the loyalty of holidaymakers. Their names alone conjure a fantasy world of exotic temptation.

Seaside entertainment spanned a wildly varied spectrum. There were simple, traditional amusements such as itinerant one-man bands, minstrels or Pierrot shows acted out on makeshift stages on the beach. But there were also thrilling rides based on the latest engineering technology and everything from ballrooms to bandstands exhibiting an architectural flamboyance rarely seen elsewhere. There were concert and dance halls (a descendent of the original Georgian assembly rooms), aquariums, cinemas, restaurants and tea rooms, neatly laid out gardens; tennis courts, boating lakes, roller rinks, crazy golf courses, amusement arcades, playgrounds and of course fairgrounds.

The introduction of amusement arcades was inspired by the pleasure beaches and piers in North American resorts, notably Coney Island. William George Bean, founder of Blackpool Pleasure Beach in 1896, envisioned a place, 'to make adults feel like children again and to inspire gaiety of a primarily innocent character.' This was exactly what fairground rides from roller coasters and log flumes to flying machines and joy wheels did, reducing usually staid and sensible adults to giddy, giggling wrecks; leaving them in a delightful state of disarray that would be considered unseemly in everyday life. But the seaside was a place where the usual behaviour codes could be left behind at home.

Some seaside visitors preferred less visceral entertainment; perhaps a restful stroll in one of the carefully manicured municipal gardens that peppered the seafront, taking tea in a palm-filled tea room or an afternoon spent in a deckchair listening to the strains of a military band oom-pah-pah-ing from an elegant bandstand. Families were well served by sandy playgrounds, miniature steam trains (essential for any resort) or, considered wholesome family fun at the time, beauty pageants held in one of the huge swimming lidos built between the wars. Wide, open seafront esplanades were perfect for pedal cars and novelty seaside pushbikes and go-carts.

The British seaside's rapid decline at the end of the last century left some of its resorts' once grand pleasure palaces in a pitying state of decline. But there are signs of renewal. Margate's Dreamland has been sympathetically returned to its former glory and re-opened to great acclaim. Spanish City in Whitley Bay has received lottery funding to be restored and re-imagined as a leisure facility and wedding venue. Whether these examples of seaside regeneration are part of a swelling renaissance remains to be seen, but it is gratifying to witness these ghostly edifices ringing with music, screams and laughter once more.

The magnificent Tower Ballroom at Blackpool pictured in the 1930s by the artist Fortunino Matania for a Blackpool Tower and Winter Gardens souvenir programme. Designed by theatre architect, Frank Matcham in a staggeringly opulent style, the ballroom opened in 1899 and has been a mecca for ballroom dance enthusiasts ever since, keen to dance upon the 37m x 37m sprung dancefloor of mahogany, oak and walnut. Matania's painting, showing spectators in the balconies enjoying refreshments as they gaze upon the crowded dancefloor below, conveys the scale and baroque splendour of this iconic venue.

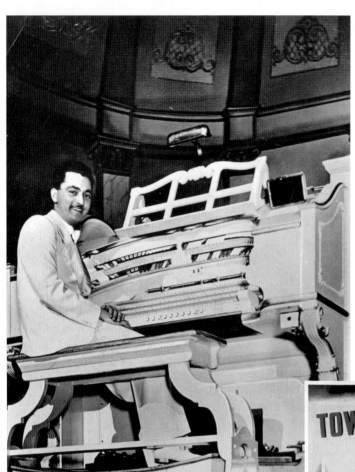

10931089 –'Mr Blackpool' aka Reginald Dixon, resident organist at the Tower Ballroom in Blackpool from 1930 to 1970 and a regular on BBC radio. The ballroom's original Wurlitzer organ was installed in 1929 but was replaced with one designed by Dixon himself in 1935.

1938 souvenir programme cover for the Blackpool Tower & Winter Gardens, listing the dizzying array of entertainments on offer from the Grand Theatre to the Empress Ballroom.

Not all ballrooms could boast the lavish interior of Blackpool's. Here, the 'ballroom' in the Ormescliffe Hotel, Llandudno offers a more modest experience in the 1960s.

Blackpool's famous illuminations first lit up the seafront in 1912 in honour of a royal visit, has continued through the years to attract visitors and extend the resort's season from late August to early November. Though other seaside towns introduced their own illuminations, notably Southend and Llandudno, Blackpool's remain the preeminent must-see display every year.

View of Connaught Gardens at Sidmouth, East Devon, showing the carefully-planted flower beds. The gardens were named after the Duke of Connaught, one of Queen Victoria's sons, who formally opened the Gardens on 3 November 1934. Pleasure gardens offered visitors to seaside towns a tranquil place to stroll, away from the beach and seafront, and many towns invested in municipal spaces mindful that such attractions would increase a resort's appeal. This photograph was taken in the Edwardian period by Reginald A. Malby (1882-1924), official photographer to the Royal Horticultural Society.

The Palace Grounds, Clacton-on-Sea, from a postcard dated 1908. The Palace-by-the-Sea opened in 1906 and its pleasure gardens boasted such exoticisms as the Blue Caves of Capri, the Neopolitan Pergola and a Japanese pagoda.

Edinburgh Marine Gardens, Portobello, Scotland. Marine Gardens Pleasure Park was constructed at Seafield, Portobello in 1909, using many of the buildings that had formed the Scottish National Exhibition at Saughton Park in 1908. Buildings on the site included: an alfresco theatre, an industrial hall, a large ballroom, a scenic railway, a rustic mill with water wheel, and a motor cycle race track (a number of which are depicted on this postcard).

Scene at a Blackpool amusement arcade, with holidaymakers trying their luck on the One-Armed Bandits (slot machines) there. Gambling was popular with working class holidaymakers who, released from the expectations of everyday existence, found many more opportunities for casual gambling at the seaside than were available at home.

Children enjoying the 'Monte Carlo Rally' electric car ride at Dreamland Amusement Park, Margate in 1938. Dreamland, one of the country's most famous seaside amusement parks began life in the mid-Victorian era when a restaurant and dance hall, christened, rather unimaginatively, 'The Hall next to the Sea' opened in the town's disused railway terminus. Over the years the site was developed, with the first amusement rides – sea-on-land machines simulating a sailing sensation – installed in 1880. Purchased in 1919 by John Henry Iles, he opened the Grade II-listed Scenic Railway roller coaster in 1920 and continued to add more attractions, including an ice rink and cinema to the park, which was now re-named the far more tempting 'Dreamland'. In 2003, following several changes of ownership, Dreamland was closed and threatened with re-development into a retail and commercial site; thankfully, a local residents' group, determined to save this historic beacon of seaside history, have been successful. The site passed into council ownership and a newly renovated Dreamland re-opened in 2015, with design and branding carried out by Hemingway Design. Still dishing out good old-fashioned fun to Margate's visitors, Dreamland is a remarkable example of imaginative seaside regeneration and has made Margate, which can also boast the Turner Contemporary art gallery, once again a magnet for all types of visitors.

The skating rink at Dreamland, which was opened in 1893, proves tricky for one first-timer, c.1950.

The Scenic Railway roller-coaster at Dreamland providing thrilling rides in 1951. When it was opened in 1920, it attracted half a million visitors in its first year. It was destroyed by fire after an arson attack on 7 April 2008 with around twenty-five per cent of the structure, including the cars, destroyed and removed as irreparable. The restored and rebuilt roller coaster finally opened again to the public in October 2015.

A cycling merry-go-round in Southend-on-Sea in Essex, 1927.

A crowd of children gather round, fascinated by a miniature steam railway engine at Mablethorpe, Lincolnshire. During the twentieth century, almost every seaside resort around the UK had a miniature railway.

The exotic white turrets of Spanish City are a distinctive feature of the North Eastern seaside town of Whitley Bay. It was opened in 1910 by Charles Elderton who, having visited Whitley Bay with his concert troupe had keenly felt the need for an indoor entertainment complex. The resort styled itself as the 'Playground of the North' launching a proactive poster campaign in partnership with London and North Eastern Railway with the aim of attracting visitors from the south. With Spanish City its jewel in the crown, the resort thrived, enjoyed by tourists as well as the local community. Mark Knopfler of Dire Straits spent time there in his youth – the band's hit song, 'Tunnel of Love' was inspired by his memories of Spanish City. But the site gradually fell into decline in the 1980s and 90s. For some years, Spanish City stood empty and unloved – a stark symbol of the decay felt by coastal towns around the country. A regeneration project is now underway with a Heritage Lottery Fund grant enabling restoration of the famous dome.

A seaside concert party troupe in pierrot costume. Entertainers would often perform on makeshift stages on beaches, piers or seafronts where they had a ready audience. Impresario Charles Elderton's Toreodors Concert Party initially performed under a painted canvas awning to a growing audience in Whitley Bay spurring him to embark on the ambitious Spanish City project to provide a permanent venue for such entertainment.

The Virginia Reel at Spanish City, Whitley Bay. Rough, rickety and exciting, with waltzer-like turns, several Virginia Reel rides existed at British resorts around the country, including Blackpool. The first Virginia reel ride, the invention of an American, Henry Elmer Riehl, opened at Luna Park in New York in 1908. Spanish City's Virginia Reel was installed in 1925 and operated until the 1950s.

Entertainments at Southport, Merseyside including Hiram Maxim's 'Captive Flying Machine' amusement ride (which opened in 1904), helter-skelter lighthouse, figure of eight railway, and water chute. Testament to the design, the Blackpool version of Maxim's ride, which was inspired by his attempts at aeroplane design, still operates to this day, the oldest operating amusement ride in Europe!

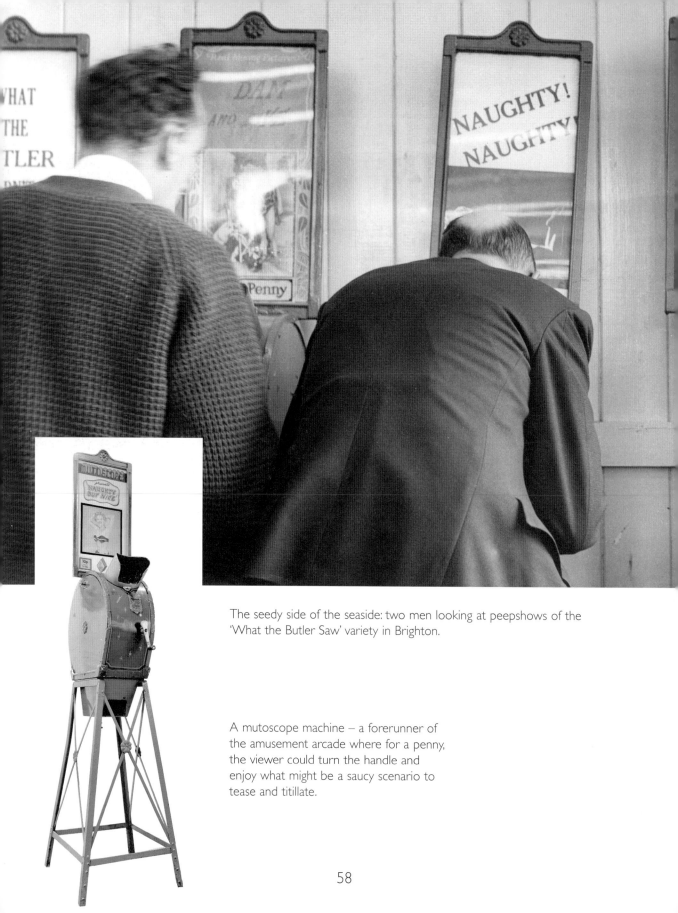

The seedy side of the seaside: two men looking at peepshows of the 'What the Butler Saw' variety in Brighton.

A mutoscope machine – a forerunner of the amusement arcade where for a penny, the viewer could turn the handle and enjoy what might be a saucy scenario to tease and titillate.

An abundant shop front in Morecambe catering for the holiday trade with buckets and baskets, postcards to send home, folding chairs, hoops in all diameters and even perambulators, c.1905.

Music sheet cover from the 1870s demonstrating how regular concerts on bandstands were very much part of the seaside experience for several generations. Many bands were German until the outbreak of the First World War. This bandstand is quite plain in comparison to many which might feature embellishments ranging from elegant birdcage scrolls to oriental details.

A wedding cake fantasy of a bandstand in Westcliff-on-Sea, 1911, drawing the crowds.

The bandstand remains an integral focal point of the seafront, though few offer the regular concerts of earlier days. This open-air concert in Eastbourne in the 1960s is particularly well-attended.

The Peter Pan Playground in Southend-on-Sea, Essex, in the 1950s. Today the site has been rebranded as Adventure Island.

Swings and roundabouts at the children's playground on the beach in Southport, Lancashire in the 1960s.

The Embassy Ballroom (built 1929), Concert Hall and Tea Gardens, the rather uninspiring-looking municipal centre of entertainment at the seaside resort of Skegness, Lincolnshire.

Piano player on Brighton beach, c.1908. A lady singer stands in front of an upright piano (perched rather precariously on some boards on the shingle), belting out a popular hit of the day. A small knot of curious youngsters and holidaying families have gathered to take in the show.

Harpist and young violin player entertaining holidaymakers on the beach at Walton-on-the-Naze, Essex, c.1900

Young tennis players rushing from the courts for lunch during a junior tennis tournament at Frinton-on-Sea, Essex in 1928. Frinton was the British resort of choice for high society during the inter-war years (a time when there was quite a craze for tennis, particularly among the middle and upper classes). Developed by industrialist Richard Powell Cooper, building was carefully restricted to preserve its squeaky clean, genteel atmosphere. Unlike its neighbour, Walton-on-the-Naze, Frinton had no pier, no pubs and no boarding houses. Instead there were quality hotels, a major tennis tournament, a palm tree-lined lido and Connaught Avenue, where exclusive shops led to it being dubbed the 'Bond Street of East Anglia'. Visitors to Frinton included Winston Churchill, Gladys Cooper and the Prince of Wales. In 1932, *The Sketch* magazine commented in its gossip column about Frinton becoming 'grander and grander'. 'I wonder they don't abolish the sea altogether, or cover it with tarpaulin, a la Centre Court, so that nobody could possibly confuse Frinton with one of those AWFUL seaside places, where concert parties and weighing machines adorn the "prom"'.

A trip to a photographic studio was one way to document a happy holiday, or not, in the case of this couple, who were captured at Read's Studios, St Peter's Road, Yarmouth in the early twentieth century looking a little glum. Note the seaside themed studio backdrop.

Far more jovial is this couple who have posed behind a seaside staple – the humorous seaside peek-through board, 1900.

Who is the fairest of them all? A beauty contest in progress at Butlin's, Skegness in the 1930s. There were numerous variations on the beauty contest including, during the 1930s, the Blackpool 'Cotton Queen' competition, open to girls from Northern cotton towns, the patriotic 'Miss Great Britain' event held at Morecambe's Super Swimming Stadium in 1945 or the Queen of Seaside Scots held at Rothesay in the 1960s.

A group of women campers about to participate in one of the myriad amusements put on at Butlin's – a wooden horse race at the Skegness camp, 1930s.

A brother and sister posing for a photograph in a truly fantastic toy car on the seafront at Brighton in 1922. The replica vehicle is fitted with lamps, suspension, a horn, roof rack and even a bonnet mascot!

Cartwright's Great Wheel – Skegness, Lincolnshire.

A jovial couple wave from a go-kart on the promenade of a seaside resort, possibly Redcar on the North East coast.

A view of the River Caves of the World ride at South Shore Pleasure Beach, Blackpool in the Edwardian era. The ride opened in 1905 at a cost of £3,000.

CHAPTER THREE
CROWDS AND SOLITUDE

'The English take their pleasures sadly,' commented French noble, the Duc de Sully of our native inability to enjoy ourselves and indeed, the crowded beaches that characterise the height of the seaside boom in the early to mid-20th century do seem, if not unbearable then at least something to be stoically endured. But in many ways, the heaving crowds and general hub-bub were all part of the holiday atmosphere engendering a sense of shared communal enjoyment among strangers. In 1949, some five million visitors thronged the beaches and piers of Britain's seaside resorts. Today, despite buds of revival and regeneration, visitor numbers are a fraction of what they were. Occasionally we get an impression of what the seaside once was; perhaps on a sunny Bank Holiday in Southend or Brighton, when the beaches are once again so crowded that deckchairs, picnic blankets and sunbathers practically block out any sand or pebbles.

The pictures in this chapter demonstrate how unimaginably popular the British seaside once was, and how 'getting away from it all' often meant quite the opposite. They show resorts the length and breadth of the country overrun with thousands upon thousands of visitors; hotels full up, fairgrounds and arcades cashing in. This was a time when the railway network visited each coastal town in the country, large and small, conveniently disgorging passengers a short distance from all the main attractions, while large groups of day trippers made their way via coach or charabanc. Despite the queues and the jostling, nobody looks sad; in fact most people look relaxed and jolly. It is worth remembering that for many, this seething, crowded experience was their one and only opportunity all year for a getaway and a break from the grinding routine of work or housework.

In contrast, remote beaches, in an era before mass car ownership, really are devoid of people. Rugged, romantic and quite empty, these places seem to offer the ultimate in wholesome pastimes for children lucky enough to holiday there. The reality might be one of bracing discomfort, but nevertheless, they conjure up an idyll which generations of parents have sought to recreate with their own offspring.

For the vast majority, the seaside was synonymous with the pier and the promenade, boisterous crowds and candy floss, big dippers and kiss-me-kwik hats. It is the seaside in all its bustling, overcrowded, garish glory. For some, the beach might instead mean freedom, solace, rock pools and lungs full of fresh air. Either way, these are elements that become embedded in our memories, stirring a strong sense of nostalgia for those golden days by the sea.

Children and terrier on an unidentified beach, 1930s

Buckets, spades and acres of unpopulated sand.

Children searching the rock pools for crabs, etc. at Beer, Devon, England, 1960s.

Running along Sidmouth beach, East Devon, 1968. Photograph by Roger Mayne.

A remote beach somewhere in Scotland, c.1920

Boys absorbed in building sandcastles on a Devon beach in 1929. Their waterproof clothing suggests the weather has kept other beach visitors away.

Wrapped up for a blustery dog walk on the beach in Devon, 1929.

Large crowd of regular August visitors to Walton-on-the-Naze, Essex, gathered together for a group photo, 1920s.

Walton-on-the-Naze looking far less populated, 1920s.

Beaches out of bounds during the Second World War. Two girls on the south coast of England look out to the beach through a barbed wire fence in 1940. Across the English Channel, the Germans were building barges for 'Operation Sea Lion', the planned Nazi invasion of Britain.

Music sheet design from the 1890s reflecting the rumbustious nature of a crowded Victorian holiday resort.

Silver Strand Wicklow, Republic of Ireland, early 1900s – a low view along the beach and cliffs with ladies and children enjoying the beach.

Holidaymakers at Cliftonville, Avon – perhaps a charabanc party, gathered together en masse for the obligatory souvenir photo of the outing.

Brighton beach packed with people enjoying good weather on Easter bank holiday, 1957; some sit on deckchairs, others directly on the shingle.

Crowded beach at New Brighton, Wallasey, Merseyside, late 1940s. The looming building in the background is the Tower Ballroom, without its tower (modelled on the Eiffel Tower as with Blackpool). It gradually decayed during the First World War and was dismantled in 1921. The complex below, which is visible in this picture, was destroyed by fire in 1969.

Beach at Newquay, Cornwall in the 1980s. Newquay today is a magnet for surfers. This crowd seem more interested in catching some rays.

Teeming sea front at Brighton, Sussex around 1950. A deckchair monitor in the foreground and a man with a religious banner makes the most of the crowds to spread his message.

Snoozing and reading newspapers on deckchairs at Margate, with sand barely visible on the busy beach below. Captured by Roger Mayne in 1957.

It's a sunny day on the
beach at Hastings,
Sussex, luckily for the
photographer
recording this group of
holidaymakers in 1912.

Margate heaving on a summer's day in the 1940s. The Dreamland amusement park and cinema can
be seen in the background.

Enjoying some peace and quiet at St. Ives in Cornwall, 1956.

A challenge to find a spot on the beach at Littlehampton, West Sussex in the early 1960s.

Southend-on-Sea, Essex, early 1930s. Southend's close proximity to London, with regular rail services from Liverpool Street station, made it one of the premier choices of destination for day-trippers.

Southwold, Suffolk, 1919.

Blackpool at the height of the summer holiday season 1970.

All human life at Blackpool in the late 1940s. Women in headscarves and sunglasses build sandcastles while a police officer looks incongruous (and hot) among the holidaymakers. Those who are peckish can try oysters, whelks or cockles from the seafood cart.

High tide at Southport, Merseyside. An ice cream seller in the foreground doesn't appear to be doing the swiftest business, possibly due to the temperature, which looks chilly from the clothing worn. In the 1924-25 directory for ice cream dealers in Southport, Robinson & Eastwood were still listed, with premises at 19a Hall Street.

Edwardian group pose for a picture on the beach at ever-popular Margate.

St. Ives in Cornwall, 1960s.

A family pose for an informal photograph on the beach at an unidentified seaside resort, c.1952. Assorted relatives are in varying states of dress from a lady in a bikini at the front to a grandmother in dress and sunhat holding a baby in a deckchair in the background. The beach is looking particularly busy.

CHAPTER FOUR

TRAVEL & ACCOMMODATION

The growth of seaside resorts was enabled by the coming of the railways in the mid-19th century, and resorts that had only previously been accessible by those with the means to afford private transport, began to find their visitor numbers soar as urban day trippers took advantage of new rail links. This development had its downsides, and the image of the raffish and rowdy excursionist contrasted acutely with the respectable long-stay visitor who could afford hotel accommodation or house rental and who, more pointedly, did not need to pack their pleasure into one single day. Accessibility was to change the character of many seaside resorts, with the most popular such as Margate and Blackpool increasingly associated with brazen, raucous pleasure-seekers, gaudy seafronts and dubious morals. The excursion train, its third class compartments packed to the gills with boisterous passengers became a stereotype; the desecration of the Sabbath (the one day working class people might have free) a cause for grave concern among more affluent and genteel holidaymakers.

But come they did and in their droves. Train travel was to ignite the seaside's rapid growth, with some railways stations, such as Ramsgate, built purely to disgorge its passengers almost directly onto the resort's sands. Elsewhere, boats sailed around the coasts of Britain, picking up passengers from city docks and dropping them at piers or jetties to begin their holiday. In the early 19th century, these were single-masted boats known as hoys – 'a strange, lubberly vessel, which staggers toward the shore' according to W. Teignmouth Shore referring to Margate hoys in his book, 'Kent' in 1907. Unloading grain at the London docks, they would return to the Kent coast laden with passengers. They were replaced by paddle steamers, a more comfortable way to travel by water. Margate, Clacton and Southend particularly saw a brisk turnover in visitors, who had embarked at Tower Bridge in London, arriving by steamer.

From the late 19th century onwards, bicycles became another popular mode of transportation with the seaside an obvious destination, and later, motorcycles, while charabancs, an open-topped forerunner of the coach became a familiar sight along

Britain's seafronts after the First World War, a mode of transport that appears comically quaint today but was once an exciting component of any group outing.

Providing accommodation for this swelling influx of visitors saw guest houses and lodgings begin to dominate the streets close to the seafront, usually run by female landladies, a much lampooned phenomenon. They catered for middle class families, providing clean, catered and conveniently located accommodation. By the 1930s, the most popular resorts could accommodate literally millions of visitors a year. Wealthier visitors could check into one of the many grand hotels which were built from the 1860s offering all mod cons from electricity and lifts to spas and cocktail bars. Some of these buildings were vast. The Grand Hotel in Brighton opened in 1864 and had 150 bedrooms. Scarborough's premier hotel, also the Grand, opened three years later and had 365, one for every day of the year. The hotel's baths offered seawater alongside fresh, and the building was arranged in the shape of a 'V' in honour of Queen Victoria. Southend's hulking Palace Hotel, opened in 1901. It boasted 200 bedrooms, a billiard room and a magnificent ballroom.

But the seaside could cater for all tastes and all pockets. The period after the First World War saw a trend towards camping and caravanning, and for wholesome living dosed liberally with fresh air. Billy Butlin recognised this and combined simple, functional accommodation in 'chalets' with the fun-packed agenda of any seaside day trip to create Butlin's holiday camps. During their heyday in the 1950s and 60s, Butlin's was where millions of British holidaymakers took their well-earned break. It was only with the advent of affordable foreign holidays that the camps, hoteliers and landladies of the British seaside began see their annual hoardes of visitors gradually ebb away.

Delightful group photograph of assorted guests at an unidentified boarding house at the seaside resort of Margate on the Kent coast during the mid-1930s. Fashionably dressed young women in the centre of the picture show off their legs and everyone looks to be having a thoroughly jolly time.

A relaxed looking chap sitting outside a tent at the Lucas Holiday Camp in Norbreck, Blackpool, 1911. The camp was a 'summer holiday camp for young men' and the location of holidays taken by the wholesome-sounding 'Health and Strength League'. It was described as 'a camp for young men of good moral character who are willing to observe a few simple rules necessary for good order'.

Neighbouring landladies, friendly rivals — Mrs Evans must be on good terms with her neighbour, for she looks on with a beaming smile as Mrs Entwhistle poses for the traditional photo of her lodgers at an unidentified resort c.1910.

FOR ME AND MY GAL.

The seaside stereotype of the dirty weekend and the matronly landlady brought together in this postcard designed by Reg Maurice, c.1922

The post First World War era saw more people travel to the seaside by independent means. Here, two young chaps pose in a Rex Motorcycle (powered by the new Blackburne engine) and sidecar on the beach at Margate.

Music sheet cover from the 1860s reflecting the great influx of day trip 'excursionists' to the seaside via train. The arrival of the masses at previously quiet resorts led to the establishment of more upmarket annexes to the main town. Thus Margate had Cliftonville, Brighton had Hove and Blackpool had Lytham St. Annes.

Day trippers arriving at an unidentified resort's railway station, c.1908.

A party of adults and children from the Aston Union workhouse cottage homes on holiday in Rhyl, Wales. They are seated in a charabanc (an open-top coach) operated by White Rose Motors, c.1919. For underprivileged children, a seaside trip in a charabanc was the highlight of the year.

Illustration by Fortunino Matania in *The Sphere* magazine, 1906 showing the New Palace Steamer, the 'Koh-i-noor' leaving Old Swan Pier in London for Margate. The Sphere described the trip as being 'the voyage down the river which brings health to tired Londoners'.

The exit from Ramsgate station channelled visitors almost directly onto the sand. View from East Cliff over the sands and railway station.

Loaded with holidaymakers, the Worthing Belle paddle steamer leaves Brighton pier for a journey along Britain's South Coast, c.1910.

The "Worthing Belle" leaving Brighton Pier.

A sketch made by *The Bystander*'s artist, Helen McKie, in the grounds of the Palace Hotel in Torquay, where, according to the magazine, 'the terrors of an English autumn and winter hold no sway … where the soft breezes and warm sunshine make this part of South Devon one of the most favoured spots in the British Isles.' McKie's sketches project the genteel glamour of the 141-room hotel on what is known as the English Riviera. Formerly a bishop's palace, it opened for business in August 1921 and boasted tennis courts, swimming pools and a 9-hole golf course. It was bombed during the Second World War while serving as a RAF convalescent home.

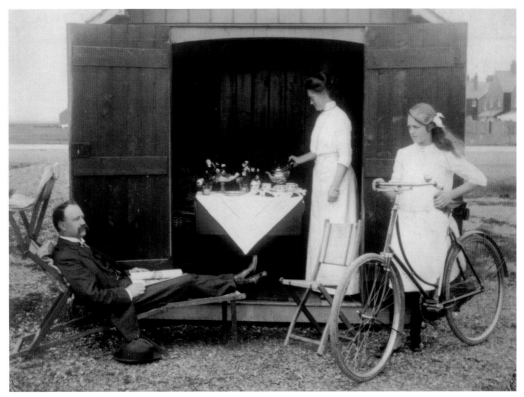

Home for the day. A beach hut at Felixstowe, Suffolk, with a family enjoying a very civilised afternoon tea, c.1910.

Guests outside the chalets at Pontin's Holiday Camp, Osmington Bay, Dorset, pictured in 1958.

Sea View Holiday Camp at Hunstanton, Norfolk, 1930s, housing its guests in rows of quaint, assorted caravans. Touring caravans increased in popularity during the 1920s and 30s and provided a flexible accommodation option for those wealthy enough to afford cars.

Canoodling couples in the back of a charabanc. Typically cheeky seaside postcard humour.

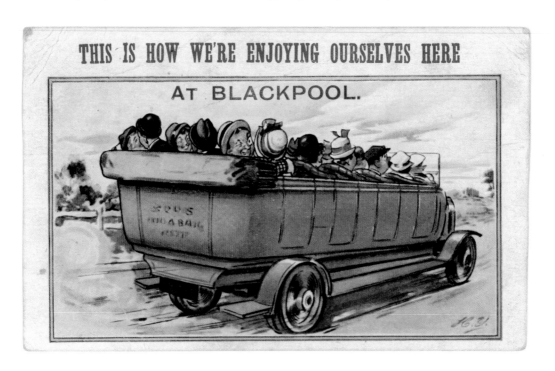

The enormous Metropole Hotel in Southend was opened in 1904 and renamed the Palace Hotel shortly afterwards. Like many large seaside hotels, it served as a hospital for the wounded during both world wars. It continues to dominate the seafront of the Essex town today.

The modest-looking Pridonia private hotel in Blackpool pictured in 1931 – typical of hundreds of small hotels and boarding houses catering to seaside visitors.

In larger seaside resorts, getting about was often done by bus or tram along the sea front. Here, men, women and children queue to board the open-top Sea Front Service bus in Brighton at a stop outside the Royal Albion Hotel.

Children play safely within sight of some cheerily decorated chalets at an unidentified holiday camp during the 1950s.

A 'B' Type Bungalow in Jaywick, on the Essex coast, c.1955. Jaywick was constructed as a holiday resort in the 1930s, with utilitarian looking prefabricated buildings offering affordable accommodation for working class families. Never intended for long-term habitation, the buildings were put into use during post-war housing shortages. Having fallen into an almost irretrievable state of disrepair, Jaywick is today classified as Britain's most deprived area.

The Art Deco splendour of Marine Court and New Sun Lounge at St Leonards-on-Sea, East Sussex. The hulking, modernist building was completed in 1938 and meant to resemble Cunard's ocean liner, the *Queen Mary*. A residential apartment block rather than a hotel, at the time of completion it was the tallest block of flats in the United Kingdom. A little shabby today, this postcard shows it in its splendid heyday, a flagship for the modernist vogue infiltrating (or in this case, dominating) the traditional buildings of British seaside towns.

Off to the seaside. A little girl waits for her train at Paddington Station, the two spades and toy yacht a clear indication she is destined for the coast.

The Carlton Hotel, Blackpool, in a prime position for visitors, facing the promenade. Though the façade has been slightly altered, the building remains a hotel today, operated by the Best Western group.

The Dining Room at The Portobello Hotel, Walton-on-the-Naze, Essex, with tables laid for a meal and two waitresses in attendance, 1956.

A group of people posing for their photo in Blackpool, next to the site of the new Embassy Hotel. A sign proclaims the hotel will have 170 bedrooms and be 'super modern'. C.1935.

In the late nineteenth century, horses were an essential mode of transport. This group of six grooms are pictured in the stables of The Marine Hotel in Walton-on-the-Naze, Essex, where guests' horses were looked after during their stay.

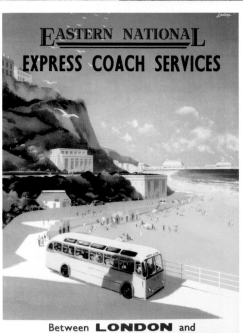

A uniform arrangement of pastel-hued caravans at the Martello Caravan Camp at Walton-on-the-Naze, Essex. This photograph was taken in 1963 from the top of the Martello Tower (one of several defensive towers built during the Napoleonic wars), which gave the camp its name. The Walton Backwaters and river can be seen in the background.

Poster design for Eastern National Omnibus Company Limited – advertising their regular coach services between London and Clacton-on-Sea via various towns in Essex. C.1950

The chalets at Butlins holiday camp in Skegness. Functional and basic, the camps nevertheless offered clean, practical and affordable accommodation for family holidays.

The Hotel Burlington, Boscombe, Bournemouth, Dorset could accommodate 200 guests. When it was built in 1893, it offered a passenger lift and electric lights – all mod cons at the time as well as a 'Winter Garden' conservatory in which guests could relax. Later, in the 1930s, it advertised its 'modern cocktail lounge.' Overlooking the bay, the inset picture on this postcard from the 1910s shows a moonlit view from a hotel room.

Butlin's holiday camps provided round-the-clock entertainment for residents in a self-contained site. Here, holidaymakers pose with an obliging elephant at Butlin's, Filey, c.1959.

Modern chalets for holidaymakers at a holiday camp in Paignton, Devon during the 1950s.

The first Butlin's holiday camp was opened by Billy Butlin at Skegness in 1936, followed by another at Clacton-on-Sea in 1938. In total, Butlin opened ten camps, eight of which were in the UK. Butlin's vision was to provide a complete holiday package of accommodation, catering and entertainment on a single site, with the 'Redcoats' he employed on hand to ensure boredom was never a problem.

A party of Blackpool holidaymakers do the circular tour of the town in an open tramway car. The Blackpool tramway, running to Fleetwood, is one of the oldest electric tramways in the world, dating back to 1885. Although the original, first generation trams were replaced by the modern Flexity 2 trams in 2012, visitors to Blackpool can still enjoy the 'heritage service', which operates on Bank Holidays and during the summer.

CHAPTER FIVE

PIERS & PROMENADES

In 1814, one year before the Battle of Waterloo, the first British pleasure pier was opened at Ryde on the Isle of Wight. Designed by John Kent of Southampton, the pier was 2000 feet long and was extended in the mid-19th century to accommodate an adjacent railway and tramway track, 'to meet the steamers that land holiday crowds as well as passengers for all parts of the Island.' (*Isle of Wight* by A.R. Hope Moncrieff, 1908). Ryde's pier was the first of many. By the turn of the 20th century, around 100 piers existed in coastal towns around the country offering a compelling selection of leisurely activities and amusements for visitors, who were seduced by the novelty of experiencing all this fun above the waves, and often some considerable distance from the shoreline.

The pier phenomenon highlights Victorian engineering at its best. One of the most prolific seaside architects was Eugenius Birch, who designed fourteen piers in total including Blackpool's North pier and Brighton's West Pier. Birch, who had spent much of his early career as an engineer in India, showed the influence of his travels in many designs such as the Pavilion on the North Pier Blackpool, inspired by the Hindu temple at Binderabund while subsequent piers, by Birch and others, exhibited increasingly varied styles of architecture ranging from Gothic to Moorish, all with the aim of providing an escapist fantasy world in which visitors might part with their money. And there were plenty of places to do so. Theatres, dance halls, fairground rides, concert halls, booths, cafes, restaurants, aquariums, cinemas and camera obscura were among the enticing delights crammed onto these platforms in the sea. Some of the integral buildings were immense considering their location. The Birch-designed pier in Hastings, for instance, included a pavilion with seating for 2000.

One of the appeals of the pier, and the seaside in general, was the opportunity for a simple stroll, along the 'promenade' and in this respect, the pier was an extension of the esplanades and seafronts along which crowds of visitors would amble and meander, enjoying the sea air and views. The architecture and aspect of these pedestrian thoroughfares became the subject of many a picture postcard –

with seating areas, benches, shelters, deckchair attendants and refreshment kiosks all appearing at regular intervals to offer rest and sustenance. Walking, for its own sake, rather than with a particular destination in mind, was thoroughly encouraged at the seaside, with town planning and landscaping focused on providing pleasant places to do so.

The one hundred piers that once embroidered Britain's coastline have now been reduced by half, the victims of neglect, dereliction, vandalism, storms or fire. The skeletal West Pier in Brighton, destroyed by fire in 2003, is a haunting emblem of the seaside's fluctuating fortunes. In 2014, another great Birch pier – Eastbourne – was also destroyed by fire. Margate Pier, Birch's first design, was damaged irreparably by a storm in 1978 and eventually demolished. But many remain, and although the attractions may be less genteel, the pier remains a magnet for modern day visitors and an inimitable and idiosyncratic symbol of the great British seaside experience.

The Lynton and Lynmouth Cliff Railway pictured in 1905, saving visitors a steep walk down to the sea. Appearing in the mid-Victorian era, funicular railways at the seaside not only offered a practical solution to accessing the beach down steep cliffs, but became a novel attraction for visitors. Other funicular railways include Saltburn, Bournemouth (the world's smallest) and Hastings. With high cliffs separating Lynton and Lynmouth on the North Devon coast, its cliff railway connected the two and opened up both to visitors arriving by paddle steamer from Bristol and Swansea. Its inaugural journey took place on Easter Monday 1890, and it continues to carry people up and down the cliffs today.

At 1.341 miles long, Southend's pier has stretched into the Thames Estuary for over a century, and remains the longest pleasure pier in the world. The original pier accommodated a narrow gauge horse tramway to convey goods to the pier head and, when the pier was rebuilt in 1890, an electrified track enabled a train to transport passengers up and down its length. By the 1930s, four trains with seven coaches each were running on a double track.

A jolly quartet of friends, arms linked for a photograph, while on holiday in Margate in the 1930s. The chaps are in casual wear (defined by the open collars and sporty knitwear), the girls are in summer dresses and hats. Deckchairs for lolling and sunbathing can be seen to their left and to their right, a lady is getting her chocolate fix from a Nestlé's chocolate dispenser machine.

A smartly turned out family enjoying a seaside outing in Margate in 1936. Mother is fashionably dressed in a white sporty dress with beret, and the little boys are wearing identical outfits of berets, jackets, shorts and sandals. Not to be outdone, father is in a light suit with knitted waistcoat and white casual shoes. Armed with buckets, spades and a ball, this promises to be the perfect day on the beach.

Margate Pier, pictured around 1900. Opened in 1853, though not completed until 1857, Margate was the first pier to be designed by seaside architect Eugenius Birch. Originally intended as a jetty for passengers landing from the paddle steamers bringing visitors from London, the pier was substantially extended in 1875 with the inclusion of an octagonal pier-head and pavilion. The pier suffered extensive storm damage in 1978 and after several attempts at demolition, was finally dismantled in 1998. Remains of the pier can be viewed in Margate Museum.

The UK's earliest pier in Ryde, Isle of Wight. View of the town from the end of the pier, taken from Nelson's *Isle of Wight*, 1850s.

The West Pier in Brighton, West Sussex, 1923. Designed by Eugenius Birch, this was the first pier in Britain to be given Grade I listed building status. The pier received two million visitors during the years of 1918 and 1919, but shortly after the Second World War its popularity began to decline, leading to its eventual closure in 1975. Having suffered a series of devastating fires during the early 1990s, only the skeletal remains of the West Pier continue to stand off Brighton's seafront.

Rhyl's many visitors are seen enjoying the landscaped gardens along the promenade as children happily zip along on rented tricycles during the summer of 1933.

Douglas Promenade, Isle of Man 1897. Constructed in 1878, the Loch Promenade was a worthy edition to the seafront of Douglas, having been constructed with the intention of attracting more holidaymakers to the Isle of Man. In 2013 a major regeneration scheme of the seafront began as the promenade had suffered serious neglect in the decades previous to this.

Visitors seen crowding together on Redcar's esplanade to enjoy the Punch and Judy show played out on the seafront. Redcar grew and thrived as a seaside resort following the arrival of the Middlesbrough and Redcar Railway in June 1846. The resort attracted tourists from nearby Middlesbrough and Stockton-On-Tees who found Redcar the perfect getaway from the heavy industry of Teesside.

Clacton-on-Sea, 1947, the town's Central Promenade featured a swimming pool and theatre which proved very popular with the holidaymakers who flocked to the resort in the early twentieth century.

Gravesend, Promenade c.1950; a group of children look out over the Thames Estuary. Due to the close proximity to London, the town saw many of its visitors arriving via the short railway journey from the capital.

Filey, 1901. Parasol-clad holidaymakers stroll along the seafront promenade in this Yorkshire resort. Filey proved popular with visitors from the busy neighbouring seaside resort of Scarborough looking to seek solace in the comparative peace and quiet.

Hastings, Sussex c.1915. Huge crowds promenading along Hastings Pier. Built in 1872 and designed by Eugenius Birch, the pier boasted many attractions and facilities such as a 2,000 seater pavilion and a camera obscura.

Brighton, c.1962. A group of elderly women enjoy a relaxing sit-down following a Sunday afternoon stroll on the promenade.

Beach packed out with holidaymakers near the splendid Grand Pier at Weston-Super-Mare c.1950.

A young couple look out to sea from York Terrace, Sidmouth's busy promenade c.1924. The seafront Georgian villas are a fine example of how the town prospered as a fashionable seaside resort during the nineteenth and twentieth centuries. Queen Victoria spent time in Sidmouth as a child and it was here that her father, Edward, Duke of Kent, died in January 1820. Many of the town's streets and thoroughfares are named for its royal connections.

Bournemouth Colonnade. Relaxed holidaymakers seated in deck chairs cast long shadows under a covered promenade supported by a colonnade of a modern design c.1950.

Worthing, Sussex, 1906. Families stroll along the Esplanade with the elegant Worthing bandstand seen in the background.

Bognor Regis, West Sussex, 1914. Ladies sporting fashionable toque hats rest a while on one of the benches punctuating Bognor's seafront.

Clacton-on-Sea, 1921. Sewing to pass the time as the sun goes down over Clacton's shoreline. Wooden shelters can be seen behind for those wishing to stay out of the sun – or rain.

8   EASTBOURNE. — On the Pier — LL.

The pier in Eastbourne, Sussex c.1900. Opened in 1870, the pier was rebuilt at a higher level in 1877 following storm damage, and due to its vulnerable location is built on stilts, which allows the structure to gently move in severe weather, thus preventing damage. Eastbourne pier has suffered from several fires over the years; as recently as 2014, the central domed building suffered devastating damage.

View of the second pier at Walton-on-the-Naze, Essex, built in 1869. An earlier pier built further up the coastline was destroyed by a winter storm in 1881, which enabled this pier to take on the business of landing and boarding passengers for the Belle Steamers carrying visitors from London. Before being lengthened, this pier was too short for the steamers to get close enough to the shore, so local boatmen used small boats (seen here in the foreground) to ferry passengers to and from the steamers. The pier was extended to its current length in 1898.

Edwardian holidaymakers along the Leas cliff path in Folkestone, Kent, linger a while to bask in the sun and take in the view over the English Channel, c.1900.

A little boy at the Bognor Regis seaside stands on the breakwater, with the shore-end of Bognor's Victorian pier seen in the background c.1920. This end of the pier held Bognor's first cinema, a rooftop garden and retail shops.

Many amusements can be seen in this photograph of Birnbeck Pier and Island in Weston-Super-Mare c.1911. Designed by Eugenius Birch, the pier includes a merry-go-round, roller coaster, swing carousel and skating rink. During the early twentieth century, Birnbeck pier was very popular with both holidaymakers and locals, though since the early 1990s it has been closed to the public and now houses the Weston-Super-Mare lifeboat station. Birnbeck pier is also unique, being the only pier in Great Britain to link an island to the mainland.

Cleethorpes, Humberside (formerly north-east Lincolnshire) c.1927. A group of strollers admire the Leaking Boot in Kingsway Gardens. The former fishing village rapidly grew as a tourist resort following the expansion of the railway from cities such as Sheffield, Leeds and Bradford. There are several 'Leaking Boot' statues around the world, showing a young boy holding one leaking boot. The original design is thought to derive from Germany while theories about what the boy represents vary from an Italian immigrant, to a boy helping firefighters.

An attendant with a bath chair 'for hire' waits for a customer to pull along the sea front at Eastbourne, early 1950s. Bath chairs, originating in Bath, were intended to transport invalids and were a familiar sight at health-giving seaside resorts in the nineteenth and early twentieth centuries.

'I'M SWANKING LIKE AN HEIRESS AT WHITLEY BAY – I'VE FORGOTTEN ALL ABOUT WORK!' Promenading was an art in itself, and for those who spent much of the year in work clothes, was a chance to show off finery and flirt with fellow holidaymakers.

Holidaymakers on the Esplanade at Scarborough, North Yorkshire, with the Spa building and bandstand behind them and the Grand Hotel in the misty distance to the right, c.1890s.

Madeira Cove, Weston-super-Mare, c.1902. This area of the resort served as a 'hub' for holidaymakers and included amenities such as a wide Marine Parade, a bandstand and plenty of deckchairs for rest and relaxation.

A group of tourists prepare to disembark on the shore of Eastbourne adjacent to Eastbourne Pier c.1910. Excursions by boat were a popular activity for holidaymakers to this seaside resort.

The esplanade in Redcar stretched the length of the entire town and was ideal for leisurely riding of tricycles such as this spectacular one in a photograph dated 1886.

Enjoying a leisurely summertime stroll along the packed Bridlington seafront in 1913.

Harry Lawrence Oakley (1882-1960), silhouette artist, pictured outside his studio on the pier at Llandudno. Oakley, whose silhouettes were in demand for posters, magazines illustrations and advertising, also cut thousands of portraits during his lifetime. He set up studios around the country, at seaside resorts and in department stores, but Llandudno was a particular favourite of his and he returned for the summer season regularly. Examples of Oakley's work can be seen in the window of his studio.

The silhouette artist, Harry Lawrence Oakley (1882-1960), pictured cutting a portrait inside his Llandudno pier studio.

Showing flesh and the latest fashions in Margate, 1930. Group of women in stylish beachwear – wide palazzo pants with vest or bikini tops – attracting the attention of onlookers as they saunter down the promenade, c.1930.

CHAPTER SIX
Water

The early seaside resorts were established in the 18th century when doctors began to take an interest in the curative powers of sea water. Several treatises by medical experts extolled the benefits of immersion in the sea including, in 1750, Richard Russel who wrote *Dissertation on the use of sea-water in the diseases of the glands* (1750). In this respect, they were the successors of fashionable spa towns like Bath or Buxton, and attracted a wealthy elite migrating to the coast to seek the 'water-cure' including royalty in the cases of Brighton and Weymouth, favoured by the Prince Regent and King George III respectively.

The apparent health giving qualities of sea bathing were counteracted by critics who claimed the activity could incite lasciviousness and immorality, the sea thought to stir all kinds of unsavoury sensations and emotion. Consequently, those who chose to swim in the sea followed strict etiquette to ensure there was no impropriety. Men and women bathed separately and bathing huts, first introduced in the mid-18th century, were designed to offer changing facilities after which bathers could descend modestly into the water without exposure to any observers. Women bathed in cloaks and dresses, men in drawers, while the voluminous skirts of the Victorians were sewn with lead weights to ensure they did not billow upwards in the water, an effect considered outrageously erotic.

By the turn of the century, swimming as an activity designed to improve overall health and fitness had replaced the notion of sea water as a cure for various maladies, and with it, the prudishness of the past two centuries began to diminish. Indoor swimming pools were opened at many resorts to provide alternatives when the weather was bad, and enjoying the water became a much more informal affair. Children might come prepared and leap around in the surf in woollen bathing suits, but the older generation often preferred a tentative paddle to full-blown immersion, with trousers rolled up or skirt hems lifted.

The inter-war years witnessed an almost cultish appreciation of swimming and, increasingly, the fashionable pastime of sunbathing. It was during this period that a number of spectacular outdoor pools – or lidos – were constructed in the art deco style, such as the Jubilee Pool in Penzance or the Super Swimming Stadium in Morecambe. Moving in synergy with this was a vogue for streamlined swimwear from brands such as Wolsey and Jantzen. The latter's tagline during the 1930s was, 'The Suit that changed Bathing to Swimming.'

Seaside resorts vied with each other to provide other watery amusements. There were boating lakes such as the one on Brighton seafront, boat trips on the sea, rafts to paddle, rock pools to explore, swimming pool water slides or amusement park log flumes. Even beauty pageants were, almost without exception, staged poolside, the shimmering water and clean lines of modern pool architecture providing a photogenic backdrop to the contestants' smiles. In less than a century, the enjoyment of water at coastal resorts had developed from a restrained activity carried out along carefully prescribed rules, to something altogether more varied, joyous and carefree.

The image of the reluctant bather was a popular one among cartoonists. This picture was published in *The Million* magazine in 1893. Note the presence of the bathing woman nearby, available to help ladies change and encourage them into the sea.

158

Sunbathing by the lido at St. Austell, Cornwall in the 1930s. The intertwined activities of swimming and sunbathing were well-established by this time, with a new interest in sport and athleticism dovetailing with the vogue for tanning. It had been a rapid development from the voluminous swimwear of the Edwardian era and the coy use of bathing machines.

Holidaymakers drying off after a swim at the lido in Blackpool, c.1950. Blackpool's South Shore Swimming Coliseum was built in 1923 on a vast scale, and was a popular venue for beauty pageants through the years. The majestic building, reminiscent of ancient Rome, was demolished and is now the site of The Sandcastle Water Park.

The spectacular Jubilee Pool, constructed at Penzance, Cornwall in the 1935 to mark the Silver Jubilee of King George V. Designed by Captain F. Latham, the borough's architect, it was kept open in the 1990s due to the actions of a local support group headed by architect John Clarke. It suffered substantial storm damage in 2014 but re-opened again in May 2016 following repairs. Photograph, c.1960.

I DON'T CARE TWOPENCE WHAT HAPPENS. THAT'S HOW I FEEL AT CLACTON-on-SEA

The carefree abandon of that doyenne of the saucy post-war seaside postcard, the roly-poly lady bather, here stepping out in a dainty little lace-up red bathing ensemble complete with obligatory garter.

1950s bathing beauties prepare for action at the Margate Lido – they seem to be partaking in some form of dressing-up game, the exact details, rules and outcome sadly long lost!

Three paddlers at Scarborough, North Yorkshire c.1915. Father has his trousers rolled up but his formal collar, tie and pocket watch chain remain in place.

Two friends at the seaside, keeping warm in their towels after enjoying a bathe in a (likely) chilly sea.

Bathers at Bournemouth in 1927 form a very British (and hence a very orderly) queue as each await their turn on the water chute.

Walley Chamberlain Oulton, Irish man of letters provided a fine picture of bathing machines in his *Traveller's Guide* of 1805. He described the roofed and walled wooden carts thus: '…four-wheeled carriages, covered with canvas, and having at one end of them an umbrella of the same materials which is let down to the surface of the water, so that the bather descending from the machine by a few steps is concealed from the public view, whereby the most refined female is enabled to enjoy the advantages of the sea with the strictest delicacy.' These magnificent examples are in position on the West Beach at Bognor Regis, Sussex.

Donkeys cool off their hooves in the sea at Weston-super-Mare, Somerset, England. The distinctive shape of the Grand Pier forms a backdrop to the scene. Opened in 1904, the Grade II-listed structure was destroyed by the fire in 2008. Donkey rides have been available in Weston-super-Mare since 1886. It is probable that the donkeys offered to ride on were originally working draught animals employed in the cockle industries around the British coast.

Children enjoying themselves in the lido next to the pier at Rhyl, Flintshire, north Wales. The lidos at Llandudno, Prestatyn, Rhos-on-Sea and Rhyl helped these towns, fearful as they were of losing tourists to Blackpool and other nearby resorts such as Morecambe and Southport, to compete for vital holidaymaker income.

The Children's Pool at The Blue Dolphin swimming pool complex just behind the Rhos Fynach restaurant in Rhos-on-Sea, Denbighshire, Wales. This nervous little lad requires the reassurance of his mother's hand as he takes his first step into the water.

Father and son enjoy an exhilarating splash in the cold surf by the Palace Pier at Brighton, Sussex, England.

Four ladies share a joke as they paddle along the water's edge at Brighton in 1957. The photographer Roger Mayne is most famous for his London street photography, but was drawn back throughout his career to the British coast and the opportunities this environment created for capturing people free from the shackles of everyday working existence.

On the Beach, Eastbourne

Paddlers at Eastbourne, with the pier in the distance, notable nearly everyone in the picture is wearing a hat, cap, bonnet or other form of headwear. The seafront at Eastbourne consists almost entirely of Victorian hotels. The Duke of Devonshire retains the rights to the seafront buildings and does not allow them to be developed into shops.

A charming photograph of an old man and his granddaughter on holiday at Blackpool. This image by Shirley Baker is part of a fantastic series of photographs depicting holidaymakers in Blackpool shot during the 1970s. Her work is touching, surprising and often hilarious, delving into the minutiae of the traditional 'British Seaside Holiday'.

Holiday makers paddling in the sea at Blackpool. A masterpiece of Victorian engineering inspired by the Eiffel Tower in Paris, the construction of the Blackpool Tower used five million Accrington bricks, 2,500 tonnes of iron and ninety-three tonnes of cast steel.

St. Anne's Beach at Lytham St. Annes, Lancashire, England. A large group of children embark on a boat trip in 1914. Early twentieth century additions to the beautiful Victorian-era Pleasure Pier at St. Annes included a Moorish-style pavilion in 1904 and a Floral Hall in 1910.

Group of men and women, all in their swimming gear on the beach at Scarborough, North Yorkshire, in July 1914 on the eve of the First World War. Among the group is silhouette artist H. L. Oakley who is featured elsewhere in this book in later life, when he spent each summer at a studio on Llandudno Pier. The Grand Hotel is visible in the centre background.

'Looking forward to seeing you again!' Bonzo the dog sits on the beach watching a woman going into a bathing hut, and anticipates what she will look like when she comes back out! Bonzo was first created in 1922 by the British artist George Ernest Studdy. The perky pup quickly rose to fame in the 1920s, starring in one of the world's first animated cartoons and becoming an inspiration for early mass-marketed merchandise. The seaside, with its cheeky possibilities, was a popular theme with Studdy.

LOOKING FORWARD TO SEEING YOU AGAIN!

Pictured in front of his bathing machines on the beach at Walton-on-the-Naze, Essex, c.1910, is Charlie Bates with some of his family and the horse which hauled the bathing machines down to the water's edge and back. Holding the horse's head is Charles Polley, wearing a jumper with the title Swimming Master.

Ice creams for the girls (still sporting their swimming costumes and caps) on the terrace of a newly opened pavilion at Margate, Kent, 1926.

Enthusiastic swimmers, well serviced by a large number of bathing huts, race towards the water at Walton-on-the-Naze, Essex, c.1925.

Until the advent of manmade fibres, swimming costumes of wool or cotton regularly sagged and wrinkled. This little girl doesn't seem to mind.

Rafting at an unidentified location, 1920s.

Beautifully elaborate bathing machines from a series of lantern slides entitled, 'Bygones'. The bathing machines are clearly Victorian, but the swimwear worn by the women sunning themselves on their ledges suggest the photograph was taken some time later, around the 1920s.

A group of visitors to Cleethorpes get ready for a land to sea experience in The Sea Car, 1920s.

Boys on serious rock pooling business, 1920s

Impressive inflatable rubber ring in the shape of a duck, 1920s.

Children playing on the boating lake near the West Pier at Brighton and Hove in the 1920s. Once a popular feature of the sea front, along with the Punch and Judy show that performed close by, it was filled in by the council some years ago.

Children messing about in boats at Frinton – the high class-but-wholesome resort on the Essex coast, 1930.

BYE-LAWS
AS TO
PUBLIC BATHING

The following are the appointed Stands for Bathing Machines.

No. of Stand.	Description or limits of Stand.	Sex to which appropriated.
1	Between the Doctor's Steps Groyne and the Cart Gangway - - - - -	**FEMALE**
2	Between the Doctor's Steps Groyne and a point 100 yards to the East thereof— Before the hour of **8 a.m.** daily - - After the hour of **8 a.m.** daily - -	**MALE** **MALE & FEMALE**
3	To the East of a point 200 yards to the East of the Doctor's Steps Groyne, being 100 yards East of the Easternmost limit of Stand No. 2 - - - - -	**MALE**
4	To the West of Melbourne House Groyne— Before the hour of **8 a.m.** daily - - After the hour of **8 a.m.** daily - -	**MALE** **MALE & FEMALE**

GENTLEMEN bathing in the Mixed Bathing Ground must wear a suitable costume, from neck to knee.

Copies of the Bye-laws may be obtained at the Offices of the Council. Persons offending against the Bye-laws are liable to a Penalty of £5.

By Order,

P. E. HANSELL,
Clerk to the District Council.

Victorian prudery and officialdom combined in this notice stipulating the strict bye-laws regarding segregated bathing at Cromer on the North Norfolk Coast in 1898. Note that even in the areas of mixed bathing, 'gentlemen … must wear a suitable costume, from neck to knee.'

Image Credits

p.6, p.18 (top), p.32, p.33, p.34, p.36, p.37 (bottom), p.40, p.41 (top), p.42 (top), p.42 (bottom), p.118 (top), p.146, p.178, p.179, p.182, p.183, p.184 - *Mary Evans Picture Library / John Maclellan*

p.12, p.66, p.116, p.156 (bottom), p.184 (bottom) - *Mary Evans / IMAGNO / Austrian Archives*

p.13, p.94, p.140, p.160, p.172 - *John Gay / Historic England / Mary Evans*

p.14 (top) - *Mary Evans / Michael Cole Automobilia Collection*

p.14 (bottom) - *Mary Evans / Vanessa Wagstaff Collection*

p.15 (top), p.47 (bottom), p.49 (bottom), p.60 (bottom), p.65 (top), p.71 (top), p.71 (bottom), p.95, p.104 (bottom), p.115, p.117 (top), p.121, p.185 - *Mary Evans Picture Library/ Grenville Collins Postcard Collection*

p.15 (bottom), p.18 (bottom), p.19 (top), p.19 (bottom), p.20, p.21, p.22, p.23 (top), p.23 (bottom), p.24, p.35 (top), p.38 (top), p.38 (bottom), p.39 (top), p.45, p.46 (bottom), p.49 (top), p.50, p.51, p.52, p.53, p.54, p.55, p.56 (top), p.56 (bottom), p.57, p.59, p.62, p.63, p.64, p.72 (bottom), p.74, p.75 (top), p.75 (bottom), p.82, p.88 (bottom), p.91, p.98, p.101, p.102, p.103, p.104 (top), p.105 (top), p.105 (bottom), p.107 (top), p.109 (top), p.109 (bottom), p.110 (top), p.110 (bottom), p.111 (top), p.111 (bottom), p.113, p.122, p.124, p.127, p.128, p.129, p.130, p.131 (bottom), p.132, p.133, p.136 (bottom), p.138, p.147, p.148, p.149, p.150, p.151, p.158, p.159, p.162 (bottom), p.164, p.165, p.166, p.167, p.168, p.169, p.171 (top) - *Mary Evans Picture Library*

p.16, p.26 (top), p.27, p.93, p.171 (bottom) - *Mary Evans Picture Library / Shirley Baker*

p.17, p.28 - *John Gay / Historic England / Mary Evans Picture Library*

p.25, p.76, p.87, p.88 (top), p.89, p.170 - *Roger Mayne / Mary Evans Picture Library* p.26 (bottom), p.29 (bottom), p.47 (top), p.92, p.114, p.134 (top), p.134 (bottom), p.135 (top), p.135 (bottom), p.136 (top), p.139, p.141, p.142 (top), p.142 (bottom), p.152, p.153 (top), p.153 (bottom), p.154, p.161, p.173 - *Mary Evans Picture Library / Francis Frith*

p.29 (top) - *©Thomas Cook Archive / Mary Evans Picture Library*

p.30, p.67, p.163 (top), p.163 (bottom) - *Mary Evans Picture Library/Gill Stoker*

p.31, p.69, p.70, p.120, p.143, p.145 - *Mary Evans Picture Library / Pharcide*

p.35 (bottom), p.39 (bottom), p.46 (top), p.79 (bottom), p.96, p.181 - *© The Wentworth Collection / Mary Evans Picture Library*

p.37 (top), p.60 (top), p.81 (top) - *© Terry Parker / Mary Evans Picture Library*

p.41 (bottom) - *Mary Evans Picture Library / Heinz Zinram Collection*

p.49 - *Mary Evans Picture Library / Reginald A. Malby & Co. Collection*

p.58 (top), p.83, p.112, p.137 - *Mary Evans Picture Library / Henry Grant*

p.58 (bottom) - *© Maurice Collins Images Collection / Mary Evans Picture Library*

p.61 - *© David Lewis Hodgson / Mary Evans Picture Library*

p.65 (bottom), p.79 (top), p.117 (bottom), p.118 (bottom), p.119 (top), p.144, p.175 (bottom), p.177 - *Mary Evans Picture Library / The Pete Frost Collection*

p.68 - *Image courtesy of Finamore Antiques Dealer, Orford Road, Walthamstow, London E17*

p.72 (top) - *© PGM Collection / Mary Evans Picture Library*

p.76 (bottom) - *Mary Evans Picture Library / Sepia Images Photographic Collection*

p.77, p.78 - *Mary Evans Picture Library / Nigel Sorrell Collection*

p.80 - *Everett Collection / Mary Evans Picture Library*

p.81 (bottom) - *© National Museums Northern Ireland / Mary Evans Picture Library*

p.84 - *Photo Union Collection / Mary Evans Picture Library*

p.85, p.97, p.123 (top) - *Mary Evans Picture Library / Andrew Besley*

p.86 - *Maurice Ambler / Mary Evans Picture Library*

p.90 - *Mary Evans Picture Library / Juliette Soester*

p.106 (top) - *Mary Evans Picture Library / Peter Higginbotham Collection*